Getting Around

By Car

Cassie Mayer

Heinemann Library
Chicago, Illinois

Photo research by Tracy Cummins
Designed by Jo Hinton-Malivoire
Printed and bound in China by South China Printing Company
10 09 08 07 06
10 9 8 7 6 5 4 3 2 1

Library of Congress Cataloging-in-Publication Data
Mayer, Cassie.
  By car / Cassie Mayer.— 1st ed.
     p. cm. — (Getting around)
  Includes bibliographical references and index.
  ISBN 1-4034-8394-9 (hc) — ISBN 1-4034-8401-5 (pb)
  1. Automobiles—Juvenile literature. I. Title. II. Series.
  TL147.M375 2006
  629.222—dc22
                              2005036563

Acknowledgments
The author and publisher are grateful to the following for permission to reproduce copyright material:
Alamy pp. **7** (Transtock Inc.), **13** (Andre Jenny), **15** (Carphotos), **22** (Motoring Picture Library), **23** (Transtock Inc); Corbis pp. **4** (G. Boutin/zefa), **5** (Reuters), **10** (Douglas Kirkland), **11** (Bo Zaunders), **12** (Sygma), **14** (Michael Kim), **18** (Manfred Mehlig/zefa), **19** (Pete Saloutos), **20** (Joel W. Rogers), **21** (Joson/zefa); Getty Images pp. **6** (Adams), **8** (Hall), **9** (McLain), **16** (IPS), **17** (Johner).

Cover image of a car in Cuba reproduced with permission of Bob Krist/Corbis. Backcover image of a Volkswagen Beetle reproduced with permission of Reuters/Corbis.

Special thanks to Margo Browne for her help with this project.

Every effort has been made to contact copyright holders of any material reproduced in this book.
Any omissions will be rectified in subsequent printings if notice is given to the publisher.

Contents

Getting Around by Car

Every day people move from place to place.

Some people move by car.

How Cars Move

wheel

Cars have wheels to move.

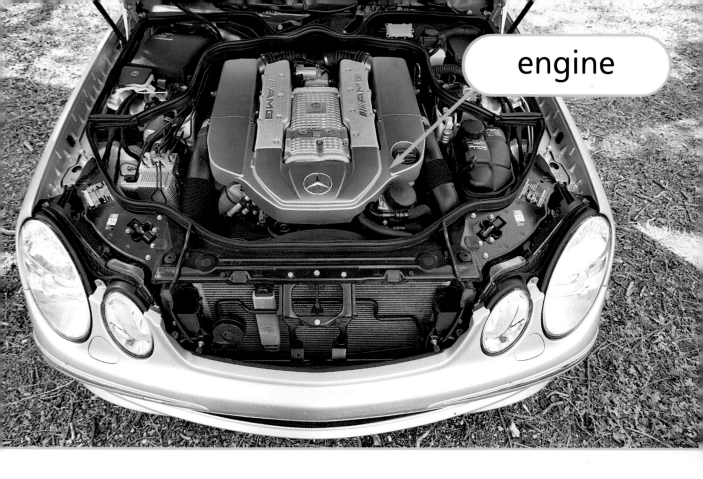

engine

Cars have an engine to move.

pavement

Cars ride on pavement.

Cars ride on dirt paths.

Types of Cars

This car is big.

This car is small.

This car is long.

This car is short.

This car is fast.

This car is slow.

Where Cars Go

Cars ride through cities.

Cars ride through the country.

Cars ride through deserts.

Cars ride through forests.

Cars can take you to new places.

And your feet can do the rest.

Car Vocabulary

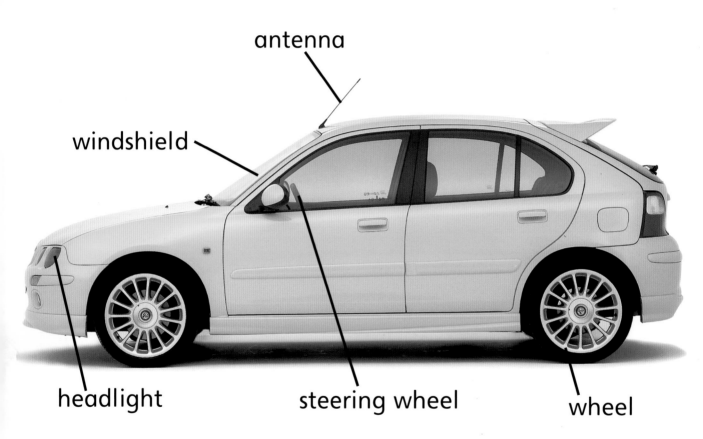

antenna

windshield

headlight

steering wheel

wheel

Picture Glossary

engine a machine that makes a car move

Index

Notes to Parents and Teachers

Automobiles are a form of transportation familiar to children, but how are cars used beyond their own neighborhood? The photographs in this book expand children's horizons by showing how people throughout the world move by car. Some of the locations featured are New York (page 16), Indiana (page 14), Washington (page 19), India (page 4, 6), Mexico (page 5), South Africa (page 9), Cuba (page 10, front cover), Portugal (page 11), Japan (page 12), France (page 13), and Namibia (page 18).

The text has been chosen with the advice of a literacy expert to enable beginning readers success reading independently or with moderate support. An expert in the field of early childhood social studies education was consulted to ensure developmentally appropriate content.

You can support children's nonfiction literacy skills by helping them use the table of contents, headings, picture glossary, and index.